STRAIGHT AHEAD

POEMS

RED SHUTTLEWORTH

BLUE HORSE PRESS REDONDO BEACH, CALIFORNIA 2017

STRAIGHT AHEAD

RED SHUTTLEWORTH

Blue Horse Press
P.O. Box 7000 - 760
Redondo Beach,
California   90277

Cover art: Luke Shuttleworth,
"North of Soap Lake" (2016)

Editors: Jeffrey and Tobi Alfier
Blue Horse Press logo: Amy Lynn Hayes

ISBN 978-0692809976

Acknowledgments:

The poems in this collection were first presented, some in slightly different versions, on my blog: poetredshuttleworth.blogspot.com.

The sequences (except for *Straight Ahead*, which is new work) were subsequently issued in limited edition chapbooks from Bunchgrass Press.

Special Thanks for Counsel and Editing Advice:

Jeff and Tobi Alfier, J.V. Brummels,
Barbara Brinson Curiel, Nuno Santos,
Ciara Shuttleworth, Kris Wetherholt,
Paul Zarzyski and Elizabeth Dear.

In Heart and Thought:

Bridget Clawson, The Devlins, Carol Gabriel,
Al & Nancy Gallagher, Gary & Michele Gildner,
Julie Jensen, Dave & Sylvia Kelly, Toni Loppnow,
Loughlins, Johnnie & Patty Phillips, Jessi Shuttleworth,
Luke Shuttleworth, Maura Shuttleworth,
and Patrick & Jaquith Travis.

In Memoriam:
Jerry L. Crawford.

For a Long Mystery:
George Lovel Manley

For

Kate

Contents

Just Under a Hundred Degrees

Gold-fire afternoon light....

You slow-drive,
dried blueberries
instead of Copenhagen,
stretch an hour on a gravel road...
gape-grin dumb
across sagebrush
at not-so-distant basalt walls.

As if there ain't nothin'
you can't dream up for real.

Rambling Apparition

Rambling Apparition

1.

You move under a black full moon,
nailed-shut doors sprung open
to sunflower-tinged dying clouds.
You rise from pillows stuffed
with serpent bones, no grip for jewels.

2.

All the certitudes of August, baled in straw,
claw manic toward sunshine: lost painted
mouse skull, silver crucifix necklace, badger rib.
All you have against time-wrinkled decades
runs thick and dark in the arteries, like pine tar.

3.

No charity liquor store bottle.
The sky is full of slick-dust moon
craters marbled with fake rivers.
Gravel takes your pulse as you fall.
Why not replace windows with cow hides?

4.

The desperate kiss of lovers...
four-inch thick glass between them.
The graves of grammarians below sidewalks....
A sunrise bird hurtles breath-short off a windshield.
Oh... finality of clenched-fist clouds and clay urns!

5.

Smoke from grass fire... caught for a ride
on a dragon-plume wind. Church mice playing
tag in a bundle of yellow choir robes.
A convulsive two-lane blacktop... a man eating
a dog-hairy sandwich, elk haunch with mustard.

6.

Let the arteries scold you later,
let wind-slanted pines wait for feathered lightning.
You tilt your head, squint an eye as if facing a bald sun,
gnaw summer's bloody bone for what meat is left.
Slurp and gulp water from a silver pail... laugh!

7.

Garden and porch roses, like runny ointment
for fly-bitten summer holiday skin.... But purple
flowers from beside cursed rock and sagebrush....
Honey and white mulberry tea on a lunar morning:
you are closer to the once-feared stone gate.

8.

Spectral memory: the rattle of age-chipped dice
in a thick leather cup... the fate-toss onto a zinc-
plated bar. You are barb wire-fastened to groan-
reunions, dust devil swirls where desert wind
ever-grinds the slim-familiar from any mirror.

Heart Over the Edge

In Memoriam
Wolfie Shuttleworth
May 15, 2007 – January 4, 2013

Heart Over the Edge

1.

It is the calm before sound is swallowed
inside a no-jostle abandoned movie house.
Twilight thunder as Roy Rogers chases
addled rustlers across a blank, torn screen...
trailed hard by flattened popcorn boxes.

2.

Hard frost, luminous birch trees on parade,
freeze-dried sunflowers... petals too sharp,
too crisp to play *she loves me – she loves me not.*
Low-to-the-ground pine bush, snow flurries: blue and red
ambulance lights stain a neighbor's farmyard.

3.

Rock-strewn small beach at a man-made
lake in the coulees: too cold to undress,
your younger woman stares at icy water.
Her skin tastes like almond paste, but she walks back
to the paint-chipped car, locks the door.

10.

Early winter's pillow-warm fringe thaws:
sunlight on pewter-blue clouds, a hair in your eye.
Winter pretends it can dance backward
in a straight velvet line... that snow-tongued hooker.
A graupel wind will soon pelt-out a blood-price.

11.

Melting November snow drips
from silk hung across farmyard night.
Weeds rub stems raw in firelight.
Water vapor off the earth's scars?
A satellite whines across the sky.

12.

Thin islands of early snow: you can sing
your own short-of-breath song.
A carved-from-bar-soap pistol: gloss-ebony.
You can turn tail and run... or scrape weedy
snow into a glass, add Wild Turkey.

13.

Crumbly-rough blacktop... lonesome two-lane:
you're lumbering along, yellowed November grass
and sagebrush at each side, sort of a rolling walk,
like a Western movie actor gone to fat.
Too much has been tamed for your benefit.

20.

An east wind needles your face and you turn,
call the wolfhound back, don't even bother
to look into the drawn-down, inches-deep irrigation canal.
You know: deer, a cow or two, hurled puppies
water-flattened against grates. You swallow hard.

21.

Steep decline of temperature and firelight.
You rub your hands like a westbound Mongol
watching his horse drink from a half-frozen river
he will not know the name of for hundreds of years.
You are a weed... blown through a time-door.

22.

You can read a hundred years of cowboy
and farmer obituaries in the brittle dead grass
around cracking fence posts. You can shake
funeral ashes from the pockets of bankers,
realtors, developers: crazy drooling at *ranch houses*.

25.

What your black wide-brim Resistol needs
is a wooden nickel hat band. What your Vegas pole-dancing
friend does not need is another maple syrup bath
under roaring neon. Meanwhile you stumble through
imaginary cinema light as it washboards a lonesome road.

26.

There's a cheap cold alone, not dirty.
Just a solitary thin-as-weak-soup alone.
You get it folding a bedspread as a favor to baby.
Or it arrives as you look at ripe-going-freckled bananas.
You can pass it on in a saloon with a sharp knife.

28.

Oblivion-silver clouds, girls jumping rope
for an audience of homemade sock dolls,
a line of low-belly cows spectral on brown grass:
the postcard dreams we mail to the truant and lost
are southward geese over a bare dirt cemetery.

29.

A poker-faced hard wind flips over
an old man's half-built retirement shack...
rolls it through sagebrush and tawny grass.
November glide... gamble-chance of bone dice.
Ice rain drags past every other day.

31.

Hazy sky... stagnant air from browned
coulees to the grimy-rapture Basin.
From any elevation, it looks
like a toy emporium's
heavily sedated ant farm.

34.

The rosy curtain of dusk falls on sagebrush,
silent as something buried-by-hand decades ago:
huddled football players, sheen of stained glass
Catholic church window saints, a parent's ashes.
You fumble-flip an old silver dollar.

36.

Up ahead an age-soiled gas can cafe, a curve of road
where April drunks sometimes disappear into a flood lake,
an abandoned farmhouse broken by a dozen winter-grips....
Winter sunlight on alfalfa stubble, a stranger's gaze:
erasure-by-time gets married to graveyard dust on the tongue.

49.

Thin sleet every half hour... silence,
spectral sharing... gifts of darkness.
Almost daybreak... and the aftertaste
of pork and beans at a campfire.
Edward Munch's worms are eating stars.

76.

A heaving, sweaty uphill, at last light.
You gulp bottled water. Death is a black iron
cake you will taste if you step on a loose rock.
The Wolfhound belly-laughs, rounds a boulder:
Would you believe I'm Randolph Scott in a Western?

79.   (*To the Memory of Ron Lyle*)

A friend dies in November and you get
the sharp-blade word a month later.
It doesn't matter how many guardrails
are put up. The heart goes over the edge.
Brick-fisted, he blood-earned his seventy years.

80.

Follow rusty barb wire fences
or a slick high desert road at eighty-five.
Tarps over alfalfa bales stacked three-stories high.
Antique pistols under the pillows of scrape-by-ranchers.
Regrets are browned lettuce leaves saved for just-in-case.

85.

Flowering red-hot tokens of blister-proof hope:
the New Year's Eve fireworks of town, sixteen miles away,
nest and break nest in a splendor-black sky.
The moon yawns at earthly thud and bang...at human hope.
From the rocky plateau: a bloody-tub dawn sun will rise.

88.

You spill a sack of frozen blackberries
on the kitchen table. They resemble gone-years,
the disordered-firewood ones, the ones you
curate within coiled barb wire, the ones that baffle
you with love and hard departures of love.

90.

The moon's crushed-rock, pocked face
is plenty to tangle your brain in this
halfway-through-winter. You trudge
a near-frozen creek, return home with chills.
You want any available vice to warm you.

104.

Ice-stippled ground. Wispy clouds thorn-fly
eastward between you and a porcelain moon:
revved-up memory of the U-Haul eighties…
bank-broken farm families, kids clutching
butter sandwiches, driving bare-boned for Vegas.

115.

There are other places, not so tumble-far off,
with snow tonight, not too roadside-cafe closed,
perhaps warm inside log and glass cabins in mountains
that annually catch a Cessna or two against a tree line.
Ice rain falls to stitch-close paved road traffic.

117.

A shroud of ice-crust snow rolls before you
like vanilla-white cake topping… or a sheet,
spare the lace tablecloth, over a corpse.
Yet… the beauty of January stars sparkling
across a farmyard toward a sun-gold horizon.

125.

When you look close at bygone years,
they dissolve... and the air forms ice crystals
on the elm you mowed and weed whacked
until your youngest daughter said, *No... that is a tree.*
Error and loss: in silver years, you smile.

129.

There is room for a snowy basalt evening...
lonesome skin of dry grass and sagebrush.
The ghost of a turquoise horse rises
from distant smoke. It is human absence:
silence rushes through you like molten rock.

134.

For Sale by Owner / No Hunting: You have checked
that sign-posted triangle of snake ground for decades.
It's a roadside orphan. This morning, no traffic,
you fire six pistol rounds into patches of melting snow.
Signs and rattlers have taken enough winter punishment.

135.

Slick roads before a noon thaw. You start
to think about cheap motels of the American West:
thin walls and orgasm-moans, curtains stained
with maple syrup, paintings of rotten fruit,
drunks freezing to death in empty stock trailers.

152.

Midnight and the sound of your neighbor's
new cows learning where his electric fence is.
Wet snow is falling in families... not flakes.
White-headed old man, you're still living out
a strawberry-sweet ticket: coyote-heart bliss.

Coyotes Singing Scabby

Coyotes Singing Scabby

1.

You stretch north for a first morning freeze,
Drive to a slow-pulse border, pines attacked
by the gypsy moth, henna-haired women in bars
sulky at self-fabled youth. You are rusty
barb wire with an exaggerated shadow.

3.

The sun's black shadow gulps air.
A coyote runs mannequin-stiff
past a car-clipped roadside cat.
The beast of drought, wildfire,
offers carbon autographs at sundown.

4.

Desert moon or moon-bent cold night,
your gravel road calculations sparkle
in a Wolfhound's eyes. Familiar ghosts
despair and strain in loneliness sweats.
You grope for a wind-broken barb wire fence.

8.

Diminished distance: timber fire ash falls
sunrise-soft on the roofs of cars. Flask whiskey
and arterial blood, cocked head of a Wolfhound
as you point out the last vanilla-white morning star:
madness of a horse joked-into a hotel room.

15.

The heart knots-up, locked into the bittersweet
melancholy of a ghost town rodeo arena...
a splinter-crumble pine barn behind the chutes.
Unreal gray ponies, ancient coiled reatas:
1964's rodeo queen rips sour lottery tickets.

17.

Decades of burned-black thin steaks,
chilled rattlers squeezing into October cars
for a shadow of warmth, polished aluminum
mirrors and empty pint-bottle restrooms:
you're old as a boarded-up desert cafe.

19.

Too-narrow-to-turn nothingness roads
within copper-glow of a Coke-colored
sinking sun: oh, to belt out a love song
at one's own funeral! The miles we log
should be for love and lust: pink panties.

20.

Lermontov calls from the mansion of autumn
where he polishes silver-plated dueling pistols,
where Marilyn happy-dances waist-deep in transparent
diamond-rippling water.... Does it lemon-pie-matter
if there is no such star-glitter heaven for the melancholy?

22.

Whiskey to square-up the shoulders!
You have stiff-vowed to oil paint your way
to the month that rough-hardens you for what
is to come: October with blue jean storm skies.
Red artery-blood hell-roads... sweet solitude!

23.

Sunset like peach candle glow, sunset with burned-
salty bacon strips, sunset like a forgotten rusty plow
falling off the roof of the abundant cosmos... spinning
through eternal blackness like a washed-up athlete
in a small town bar: a love song's surprise echo.

25.

A narrow grief-room in a ghost town hotel:
no towel, a pissed-twice sheet, pine wall pegs
for a reata and an October bent-to-hell Stetson,
a hot plate for a lost rounder down to pork 'n beans.
It's burnt-grass drought air through a busted window.

31.

After a cold-water-hotel sage steppe cold day,
it's a scattered-cow-rib-bones frosty night.
Dark cobalt-blue sky, coyotes singing scabby
we-didn't-win-the-lottery songs. Black picture
frame: rusty razors and bent nails in a mayo jar.

35.

To take an ache-stretch past five years
of drought and funerals, you set the old Hermes
typewriter on the kitchen table: can it still dance?
The Hermes clacks out hard, jagged steel words
to the refrigerator's Waylon sad song hum.

38.

Faint midnight rain, perhaps a blessing
for some desert girl cutting a pale inner wrist.
Perhaps a curse for some boy driving zero-
to-ninety on a surprise-glitter asphalt turn.
October rain like a memento from Creation.

44.

No cattle shipped for half a generation,
the land waits for breast-clouds and rain.
Town surges along on skateboards,
farm auctions, a bogus voodoo shop selling
crystal pendants, posters of a devil-eyed Jesus.

45.

You work up a sweat hiking a gravel
road to a rust-weight dead truck silence,
something abandoned-foul in withered grass.
Gentle gray-black rain gathers at horizon.
October chances resemble coyote traps.

47.

Life-vinegary: night rain and your daughter's
beloved elm branch-broken by wind and down
on sage ground, gnawed by beetles.
You want to gather shreds of happiness
to your chest, card-shuffle ill-luck to distance.

50.

Iceberg movies and coffin sleep,
late night guitar twang-kisses
for wild berries or snarl of love:
a gold mythic West pitchforks
down as lightning to fry sagebrush.

52.

A sliced orange for dry mouth,
Copenhagen Snuff for dribble-'n-drool,
carcass-stink cheap whiskey
for gravel roads where the brain
strays loose and lonesome toward hell.

53.

White wing-like drapes for the dead
as they fly in and out windows,
join clouds by dark, starlings losing
themselves in the moon's marbled light.
Your hound's eyes turn rain-silver.

56.

Put a sweatshirt on the farmhouse... it's November.
Today's gritty breeze –*skin flakes of the dead* –
will bring dime-deep snow before the week
is in the grave. Rinse the shot glasses, set aside
two spoons to make stagger-racket music.

57.

Snow by dawn, yet ghost-hour grace notes:
memory of summers broiled golden...
peach ice cream, baby's lime-green boots,
beer cans in a stock tank amounting to friendship.
Fragile highway night, bright roadside basalt.

58.

A black owl sharp-turns a sky-corner,
holds for a moment to gaze-hungry
at your shuffle. You leave the trail
to the dry lake, follow the Wolfhound
to where sage riddles brain-blood.

59.

Oh... to be what is extinct upon the moon.
It's raining in Reno and the married hookers
are writing postcards home to cindery husbands.
Where you are... ghost horses shudder 'n weep,
black coulee roads turn icy with the blood of deer.

60.

Light snow on the black foreheads of cattle.
Jagged volcanic rock cliffs... a few dry coulees
to echo-breathless a graveyard north wind.
Soon darkness... then cinnamon-orange flames
to burn the fat off scratchy old poems.

61.

Four inches of cloud-wages have turned to slush,
but it's not T-shirt or haircut-warm: the southern sun
is driving an uninsured emerald-green '76 Ford Elite,
white leather interior, in the land of credit card mishaps.
You and the hound, old man, are feigning invisibility.

62.

You dream a floor of bloody rabbit pelts.
The sun has cleared snow off break-apart cliffs.
At your stumped level, you're a gape-eyed
customer trying to purchase missing memories:
moon crater jogs, pink-fire pearls in a hawk's beak.

63. (*To the Memory of Jack Gilbert*)

Perhaps he is a star now… beyond sight of Hubble,
the poet you have been trying to scratch a poem for.
What is deathbed throttle-laughter if not a Greek mask
to issue poems from as spirit gains speed-of-light?
Perhaps there is gaudy love on the new journey.

67.

The clouds blushed flower-blue and it rained
as we spoke of the death of Agrarianism,
I'll Take My Stand, and other bravado-rhetoric.
The Simplot blubber-lips, meanwhile, sprayed an inch
of poison on the land . . . built Erector Set center pivots.

71.

You're dreaming an orange sherbet sundown Western
sky over some burn-out-quick, drive-hard, barren desert,
and outside it's one November downpour after another
on coyotes at a risky road crossing. Just two days
to washed-in-shit-'n-piss, then broiled-dry turkey.

75.

The alphabet of truth needs more letters.
Compare and smile. Line up the near-thousand
months of rock-spark or no-shine life:
our days do not wait to go up in smoke.
Tonight diamond-stars crack and orgasm-glow!

79.

Mid-morning rain-glisten on pasture rock…
the reflection of a horse's eyes.
A snaky spiral of rubber-black smoke to the east.
If you act your age, your performance will take you
closer to death than to room service cotton candy.

80.

The towns and villages and hamlets of the West
fire-dance hectic… as if loaded on crystal meth.
Rest-stop-dirty communions, lovers weeping
at a December sun, emptied caffeine-pop cans:
you drive on as if through one glass pane after another.

88.

Thick, clumsy snowflakes… another heartbreak
night at the other end of the country, newspapers
tossed against crepe-black doors, blackened windows.
Cans of rattler fangs, angels on horses: tear-stained pillows.
What is the lifespan of a butterfly, of ice on a dry river?

90.

Autumn bangs a chair off a door at snowy four a.m.,
an end to clarity beyond the doped-up, dozing
Wolfhound with a bone cancer left front ankle.
He will not sing in April, not for love or burger.
What do you expect from December, indulgence?

Shrub Desert

We think that the last time is the worst.

Gertrude Stein
Evidence

Shrub Desert

1.

Mundane late summer hangs on
quirky-warm into late October.
You meet yourself in film footage
never shot, giddy with Western
yarn, half-drunk old diarist of verse.

3.

Observation of clouds, range-of-vision
from behind outcrops of volcanic rock:
light-deprivation delusions.
One auction house offers Wyatt Earp's
prostate preserved in copper mine dust.

4.

Overnight a gray northeast wind drops cold
onto the cars of men who sleep on backseats.
Russian olive trees along a half-dead creek,
stool samples left in brush, pine table legs…
spine-bone of deer: bite-lip Halloween approaches.

6.

Archival-quality volcanic rock, meteor-yellow
(off khaki) cow-cropped grass and weeds:
you dream the West (fragments gone-missing)...
crystal ashtrays from chaos motels, coyote teeth,
cheap neck rags, used-up *Gunsmoke* tropes.

10.

Black dawn... a rain-bound high desert morning...
drizzle-glazed creek side Russian olive trees,
euphoria-green like the eyes of stained-glass saints.
An actress friend, not enough make-up to smudge,
turns 47, gulps dozens of *hard candies*, emails....

11.

A break in shrub steppe showers... memory
of a sterling silver butter knife in detergent
crazy-blue as luminous afternoon rain clouds.
You beg your yipping skull-coyotes to cease
whiz-bark-whirl, to hush poem-bruised tongues.

13.

Jack-o'-lanterns a few hard days removed,
light desert snow drips onto a new graveyard.
Our days grim-sparkle with manic garments,
chewy-gum, blue aluminum charms
for emo jeans . . . tabloid-stuffed bikini tops.

14.

Silver skull sky, temp up to 41, melting coulee snow.
Last time you bothered to look, cavorting actresses
were sputtering your mad West-nostalgia,
tin cup mezcal, mustang pretensions, carnival dolls.
A quarter century wears thin... cheap barn paint.

18.

You stumble rock-strewn barren ground,
daydream wild prairie roses... chestnut ponies.
Your stopwatch falls further behind.
Home... watercolors of shrub steppe tumbleweed,
hound-gnawed postcards and rawhide bones.

19.

A century-old wax-'n-varnish portrait....
A quarter-mile rectangle of coulee flood plain
for a lone and lonesome man to locate himself on...
a 19th century railroad hotel busted to splinters.
One day a man dies: drizzle and ghost guitar.

20.

You can count on the romance of running away,
right into the blindness carnival barkers
look for in prey. Dusk falls like a gray beard
onto a freeway cafe's cigarette-scarred counter.
Faint blues, off-golds: headlights against darkness.

21.

A purple hue to the sky... like horsehide in a movie,
and time falls with loose rock from ancient plateaus.
A'horseback you pay attention to what is inside...
the formation of dreams within extinct volcanoes.
There are men in rest homes who double for themselves.

22.

The faded colors of November shrub steppe grass,
lunatic-khaki and horse-piss-yellow, match the cruelty
of country singer ghosts placing clear plastic bags
over each other's heads... rivalries even in Heaven...
pewter-fluorescent faces... like rainy day gravel.

23.

Mid-autumn high desert fog... just above
freezing memories of jasmine-July blondes,
sun lotion, breast sweat, jeans and tank tops
piled near a bonfire. Shrub steppe ice fog:
moody morning... a phone buried under sage.

25.

Scissors from a drawer... you cut open
a sack of frozen strawberries, spill them
like spirit notes across a dog-gnawed table.
Time passes . . . November monologue...
wind through porous stone and bunch grass.

26.

Tales of carnivorous rock, pencil sketches
of wing-shot, exhausted wagon train angels...
reconstituted-with-shale outlaw blood
pooled on crumble-prone desert blacktop....
Catastrophe-hints tick slow... stolid minutes.

27.

Gravel road trajectories... milestones....
You're floating behind some luminous action.
Or you're off stage... listening for your cue.
Full attention is a melancholy tumbleweed.
You've not bought town clothes in a decade.

30.

You take a postcard-expansive view,
drift the coulee steppe... happy as an ancient
jeweler finger-walking a ruby-secret vault.
You delight-stumble on a washboard track:
cloud of starlings, a time-broke cedar post corral.

31.

Pewter-vibrant sky... and you are hard-grounded,
perpetually preceding yourself in dreams:
bronze sculpture coyotes, charred log cabins giving way
to upside down, hide-stripped bison, to Conestoga-borne
movie extras headed ever westward with manic songs.

32.

A cerulean-frost coulee country morning sky:
you juggle a chunk of basalt,
squint and daydream red oxide Utah...
busty Shakespearean actresses in Cedar City
hawking fresh-baked strawberry tarts.

35.

You are no stranger to icy fog,
purported heavens... man-made lakes
with rock-strewn shorelines: ghostscapes.
No bird flies through ice, no hound returns
from the dead, not a dim light on the far shore.

If You Had a Tail Fins Caddy

Fiasco dream....

Wyatt Earp
(Staring into the Mojave Desert, 1925)

If You Had a Tail Fins Caddy

1.

It is raining hard on this high desert,
glossy as curated queen-skull.
Summer comes tomorrow like Johnny Cash
on old time radio, wired-tight on a dangerous
prescription of mourning, kisses and prayer.

6.

A busted-up old corral and scrubby pasture
remind you of pain-worn lovers nursing
watered-down drinks. The neighbor lady
reckons it's bleeding outside, stays indoors.
It's an ash-blue crop duster morning.

15.

Dusty boots and stone-pillow naps,
you are falling further into Old West
caricature... no longer brick-fist-quick,
no longer chased by baton-toss princesses.
The clouds you ride are tissue-paper-thin.

18.

The sun gouges an irrigated cropland horizon,
the foothills of the Cascades, as it dumb-falls.
And the moon is a charming old drunk
who carries an old shoe to use as an ashtray.
No wonder the ancients gnawed for bone marrow.

21.

A disordered spirit tries to whirl back
into the human niche: another dust devil
north of Moses Lake on plow-ripped
floury soil. You roll down the car window,
wait for a fuzzy ghost . . . an old friend.

24.

You slow-drive a lonesome road graveled
by the county for a joke or for practice.
After land-abandoned, what else is there?
Sagebrush, once burned for pasture,
is back, like remorse, with little wiggle room.

29.

Excuses are long distance hang-up calls.
Who's got your back?
Tour a small town nursing home
for the aged, the mad, the bestial.
Suicide is always a kind of forgery.

31.

First cutting baled, nothing like a haphazard drive
into town at peach-cream sundown... sixty on gravel,
dust-spray northward, Nashville jelly-heads singing
raw-'n-crazed from a satellite. It's a high desert,
beer-for-supper, let the center-pivot-whirl party.

33.

Horses-in-the-surf memory... a studio apartment
at the beach in sixties San Francisco... sand fleas
in the carpet... girls asking, *What should I do?*
You're aged onto lighting-prone shrub steppe...
waves of .45 Colt desperado whiskey dreams.

35.

No Wolfhound to speak with about a full moon.
No old dog, only a claw-scarred hardwood floor.
And the moon rises pale above the shrub steppe's
peach-colored dust. It is mid-July like a drunk
face-down on a stack of still-warm café waffles.

42.

Two-lane blacktop and power poles heat-warp
toward over-grazed-by-August rattlesnake foothills.
I sing Haggard... manifest myself with a roadside piss...
a mark for coyotes to make executive decisions with.
My lifescape has become all too sagebrush-filmic.

46.

Furious rain falls on week-old brush fire haze,
soaks a gravel pit millionaire's motley cattle
as they graze a center pivot home on the range.
It's a picture show rain. Lightning and thunder
eastward in power-tumbles of contempt....

50.

The unsettling birth of take-away hours...
when you drive half the night heavy-lidded
just to breathe in the smell of a Wolfhound
from the backseat's Irish ghost dog.
Porcelain-brained, you are stuck on loss.

51.

Vast expanse of sagebrush, August-dry
bunch grass, weeds, the shuffling ghosts
of Indian horses: you ride
stiff as a splintered cedar fence post.
Your song is gargled glass.

54.

A moon-white sky, ninety-six degrees at noon,
you hose just enough water on a line of pines
to keep trees alive, let the high desert keep
itself rippling-dry. If you had a tailfins Caddy,
motel free-night coupons, you'd blue-streak fly.

65.

The hard-edge enthusiasm of youth
gets left behind like coils of rusty barb wire
on aged-loose, wobbly corral posts.
Raw prophetic artistry of wind and drought:
it's best to love without looking starward.

69.

Pushed by bruise-blue clouds, wind for the southwest
trembles across the gravel road on a lacy sheet of rain.
A late August sunflower stalk flies past like a spear.
You think back on old punchy prizefighters,
raving motel maids, and railroad tracks to nowhere.

75.

Quick bloom and wither of sage steppe flowers,
windbreaks and shadow-breaks, windows down
after nightfall, a crippled hand holds a fly swatter,
another hand grips Heaney's *Door into the Dark*:
we gather… let slip our few days of whiskey-luck.

77.

You drive the shrub steppe, not far from home,
reeling at what has been abandoned at top speed:
we loved this or that horse plenty, left ranch homes
empty beyond dead yellow roses in stove-top vases,
toss coffee cans of nickels into cowboy songs.

79.

On this seldom-breeze high desert, the Cascades...
blurry foothills too far to the west to ride a horse to,
you ask your ghost, *Who're you really here with?*
A few ashen-faced clouds skitter to the north.
A blackbird, weary-rotten choir boy, screeches.

81.

Rumors of a god of rain and we sleep
naked... catalog flash-flood dreams,
roll sweaty in dusty sheets. At midnight
the farmhouse shakes with mercury-blue light.
A cinnamon coyote loose-lopes for shelter.

87.

When you stayed at the old Thunderbird Motel
in Barstow forty years ago, the tap water tasted
like a roll of nickels in an ugly girl's mouth.
Memory attacks as you lope... slip-slide downhill,
the land around you sage-lunar for coyotes and snakes.

90.

Whiskey-bolstered, you'd grin at scabland
still sage-green in September. Years gone....
You're sober these days, clumsy though,
a sun-scorched, one dog-short, thirsty
old man, blood in your glacier-water eyes.

Ice Moon

Ice Moon

1.

Bitter-howl... cold November wind.
Into the car with song and door slam,
you pull off an old blue ski mask.
The Wolfhound chortles. Tumbleweeds
rip-roll, with warm Nevada too far south.

2. (*Ominous Warmth... Colder Days Ahead*)

Fewer switchbacks as you pass seventy...
and you stare at a hyper-real desert sky:
near-invisible gray horses, darker clouds.
Fly-over jet liners. All this perceivedness
dwindling just as you wish it to blossom.

3.

Memory: frozen shirts on a clothesline...
a wreck-closed road into snowy Tehachapi.
That was winters ago... before this night...
stumble-dream over rock and icy weeds...
a slush-drip hydrant for a thirsty coyote.

4.

Frozen-hard volcanic high desert.
You daydream brass-'n-fern bars...
comet-bright fashion models reading
your poems. The illusion-blue sky
runs south, bear-mauled, half-dead.

8.

It's a yip-chant, bark-warble coyote night.
You stomp-awkward through dry weeds,
mumble, let out a laugh-distorted howl.
No moon... temperature steady at 38...
rain on its way: you're in ghost dimension.

10.

Deadpan winterscape on a shrub steppe.
Every morning you pass a Godot Tree
where it encroaches on an abandoned road.
Today dense fog... nearby spectral coyotes...
rapid-frantic bark-yips: an unbroken timeline!

13.

It'd be hard luck ground without irrigation.
Scab rock, root-starved volunteer poplars....
You daydream urban: elastic pink walls,
minimally tattooed fashion models,
pop-singer coyotes eating wine-rooster.

14.

Slight east wind... eighty evergreens,
fool-planted on coyote shrub steppe,
are soft-singing... a December cantata.
Evening carries a gold-fringe blue sky...
another dead-dog-lonesome anniversary.

17.

Dusk rain... night fog sweeps in...
you curse, slosh the December
farmyard in leaky old Tony Lama boots.
Arthritic hands, microwave box food,
postage-due mailbox-Jesus leaflets.

22.

A December creek for deer and coyote,
porcupine and skunk, before an ice-over.
A matte-gray Christmas afternoon sky. . .
you take a breath at a tumbleweed crossroad:
vagrant time, love-'n-rib-bone daydream.

24.

The last Sunday in any given year...
age-crumbled basalt... delaminated
ash baseball bats... more plastic flower
funerals than white lace weddings:
angels whine, *Just followin' orders.*

Adjacent to Heaven

Adjacent to Heaven

1.

Aged bellboy-winter leaves a last
snow clump. Dim-sunlight hours pass,
a hound's leap... and it is Spring...
bright greens and avian blues...
as if holy stained glass.

2.

Soggy ground where snow melts
around gnarled big sagebrush: you chuckle,
look for a coyote paw print, and the Wolfhound
pup runs blithely. Grittier days ahead,
but you're within the possible of spring sunlight.

5.

Nothing decorative... rain as weak-gesture
from God's ghost: the sage steppe finds spring
as small magic... splash of moss-green,
puddle-gravel roads, the hello-goodbye of lovers
stranded, sitting side-by-side on a lumpy hotel bed.

6.

Beat-up basalt pillars and light drizzle:
commonplace exhibition of dated divinity....
Decades of breakneck speed for an inner life.
Now your dreams roll out in whiskey barrels,
knock-about skits, every nap a somersault.

12.

Unpretentious cataract. The moon appears...
reappears through sculptor-ghost clouds.
Closing time for saloons in this time zone.
Your shadow pauses, a woodcut on scab rock.
The moon, wink of arctic-blue: a stumbler's charm.

16.

Austere beauty of a late March cow lot,
sagebrush against warped fence boards,
half a decade abandoned: late afternoon
pewter-blue clouds roll for Coeur d'Alene.
Fence post hawk: maybe some god's eye.

17.

There'll be midnight rain, sprinkles of it.
Coyotes will follow wobbly spring calves,
edgy young momma cows. Southeast wind,
predator bark... you're adjacent to heaven,
aged and fleshed-out, not quite pistolero.

21.

Days beyond the last tight freeze,
new holes upon a moisture-beg land:
goddamned gophers and their mounds.
A river of clouds, rumors of mini strokes,
dimpled light on scab rock: April dances.

23.

The eroded distance: fields planted
in winter wheat, alfalfa, timothy...
a sagebrush steppe hard-wrenched
from Indian ponies. Fleeting sunset...
dark hours... black tea... burnt toast.

26.

Clouds in dirty-white rodeo shirts…
supper time and shadow-dark sagebrush….
The Old West declines and crumbles
to blue rock suburban driveway gravel.
Your ivory pistol grips… cracked-'n-loose.

28.

Under the skin: the memory of a wildfire…
sage and grass smoke… a florid-red sun
at horizon. Now: film-grainy gray buttes,
an April shower, wind and sparse grass,
a gulp of bitter home-brewed Irish tea.

29.

Basalt made from nightmares of dancers…
crumble-bone and drunk-sculptor memory.
The Wolfhound charges a rock-strewn hill,
turns… blue expanse of sky behind her.
Dust devil as god… empty and detached.

31.

No geezers with metal detectors
looking for Old West artifacts...
just a quick-erode uphill two-track
to a failed gravel pit. Clump of sage
to kick through... loose-change heart.

41.

Bark-flakes... fever sweat afternoon dreams:
dark nudes in an unwritten Raymond Carver novel,
dancing scarecrows hung from Nebraska rafters,
a butcher paper sonnet in a Hermes typewriter.
Thirst rattles our empty whiskey cupboard.

47.

A broiled afternoon tips over, spills a nap dream
across a claw-gouge, dog-gnaw hardwood floor:
a lazy drive to Coulee City pushed toward another
broke-fence afternoon. You're sweaty-awake...
a shadow reminiscent of ballpark cheeseburgers.

48.

Rattler-dry inaccessible sage steppe,
assertive bunch grasses... leaning-
broke fence posts... wire long rusted:
no-irrigation desert splits from cropland.
Dust devils sing a homeward song.

Solitudes

*... perhaps it's right that we remain
essential mysteries to one another.*

Jim Harrison
The Big Seven

Solitudes

1.

You're promptly lost in black
oil paint on canvas, greeting night,
We are at five years later... every hour.
Owl on a power pole, mourning doves
flutter an Austrian pine: scrap-feather museum.

3.

Perhaps you're in a photo booth,
boots heavy with coal-gray snow...
Grete, Trakl's sister, is on your lap
after a bitter divorce. Trakl is dead.
You are a child... delivering obituaries.

6.

You're dragging a blue leather
rickety sofa down a cobble road...
equine laughter as spiritual rear guard.
It is 725 A.D. Tiny stew pot mice at-run.
Your eyes startle-open: a funerary desert.

10.

First morning of spring and no peach-glow
dawn light. Four a.m. Torment yip-barks:
coyotes lope past night-black momma cows.
Sacramental darkness, half-remembered friends
dead for years, wind-rattle of chicken-wire....

15.

Memory of a portable plastic radio,
extension cord down to a rough corral,
Hank Williams singing to skinny
Nebraska calves. The lonesome dead
so often satirize... shake the living.

16.

Carbon sky... it's snowing on an orange moon.
We are embarking on what psychic means.
Below freezing on the sagebrush steppe.
The Wolfhound listens to our observable world,
spring-dashes the farmyard in a wild lunar-circle.

17.

Clouds once ran through your hands.
You were at seven-thousand feet.
Hatched-crazy Utah... west of Beaver.
Love is such a difficult daguerreotype...
a rummage store and attic-yellow cotton.

18.

A cream-colored moon in a blue sky,
corpses stacked vertically up to Heaven....
You pop open the plastic dog kibble tub,
hardly a trailblazer in Wolfhound nutrition....
You daydream-vanish... absence of dust devil.

19.

Sublimated past... flight across
a photorealistic verdant-craters moon:
mad science... test tubes and condoms.
Stick people squiggle dance on the wall.
Fifty years back... Eros of bed & breakfast.

25.

Luminescence of long-dead stars,
grace of empty-heart prayer... its furniture
of notebook-piled desk, creaky wood chair.
And punched walls: heroes and heroines
of self-taught jigs... bison blood splattered.

26.

The appreciation of silence...
wind gusts against a window
facing a west pasture... ears double-tagged
spring calves. You take a slice of raisin bread.
Mute TV: white caps... Mediterranean.

32.

The road taken—rock and sagebrush,
owl and drought-thirsty coyote—
is a stumbler-exile's purgatory.
Load your leather dice cup,
throw the blood-red bone dice.

Amulet

Then for miles only wind.

Samuel Beckett
Eneueg I

Amulet

1.

Formerly when the stars
gathered to feast on dust....
Spill-over of tears.
Imaginary deserts call you
to ride a rag-effigy horse.

3.

Wacky sky: doorknob clouds
as if there's a passage to Heaven.
South wind. Groan of a dead windmill
in a far neighbor's drought pasture:
pony bones... a few gopher mounds.

4.

Rumor of a neuro-toxic rattler
side-winding near Moses Lake,
a dead shoulder-bit Mastiff.
An old couple drops orange
tiger lilies over a fresh grave.

5.

The knowing of old railroad tracks,
like rattlesnake tremor-'n-vibration....
There are things not to wish for.
Hooked on steel, sugared on bourbon,
you repeat type, *Pistolero Rideaway.*

7.

Thin streaky clouds... like scribble...
and you have abrupt dream-shifts,
the moment enlarges: a giant bird
wings low across a sagebrushy pasture.
Whisper breeze: a hawk-dropped mouse.

8.

Half-forgotten redwood forests,
mouthful of sweet watermelon,
you sat... quipped with a dying man,
Look and *Life* pages for wallpaper:
memory... corn stubble and mud.

9.

Sixteen, quick-dispatched from school, you explore
movie posters, sneak in to Brando's *One-Eyed Jacks*,
Peckinpah's *Ride the Wild Country*, fall in puppy love
with Mariette Hartley. A poxy no-badge truant officer
near-corpses you... Coke can to your desperado jaw.

10.

Darkness protests dawn, toss of shadow,
coffee-black streak of rock on ash-ground.
Horse-gaze, fading distant lights of town,
tangles of rusted barb wire and cedar posts....
Along with a hope-dream comes charcoal.

11.

Dozed the better part of a hot day,
dreams spiked with dental offices:
entropy lurks in ancient wisdom teeth.
No formidable rattler at evening's door,
no paired missionaries... only desert pines.

12.

Today's clouds cobble-up a storm for mountains
past Spokane. Another old wisdom tooth gone...
shattered on a dentist's tray. Your jaw swells
to meet darkness. You drive with brights, honk
at Limousin heifers... moonlight dumb on gravel.

13.

Hallucinatory desert hues, a steady onward...
no turning point: you're sitting a scorched-oak
carousel pony of prescription pain meds.
You follow a line of cracked-cedar fence posts...
wolf blood stains on papier mache masks.

14.

The fence is torn down, but a cattle gate remains:
true-life Old West fireflies outside a railroad bar.
Pioneer monuments, burlap sack frontier beauties,
antique shop postcards: in time you'll slip away silent...
clean... squared-up in a Wrangler coffin-shirt and jeans.

15.

Heap of desert grime and grease,
hideous-stained cotton, cracked buttons,
tatters of denim shirt... old man overcoat
at a spray-of-gravel, windshield glass crossroads...
as if some death-song god has staggered by.

16. *Envoi*

Burned-sagebrush... charred western horizon,
a blood-boil sun curses, hacks and sputters.

Distance to Empty

Distance to Empty

1.

Whatever is taking place, there's plenty
of blue dashboard light. Mesquite ditches,
long neck bottles, DNA tests, beef pot pie:
speed is down to zero, goddamn daydreamer.
The losing altitude juniper-Nevada years....

2.

Anguish-drives. Country radio DJ's
jangling about some day they're leaving...
dream doors blow open to blood berry trees.
December crows on-consultation. Gaelic
bronze masks laugh in the rear view mirror.

5.

No lack of December wind across sagebrush,
light rain... rough track to drive, broken-rock.
No resemblance to swollen knuckles youth
swayed by bare breasts, Cadillac delusions....
Wild Turkey... Copenhagen nerve endings.

6.

Cemetery neckties... cowboy songs...
faded *Beef State* postcards trimmed
with old scissors to fit wedding invite,
gone-yellow envelopes.... One-eyed coyote,
a whiskey-bark at a corpse-yellow moon.

7.

Pale evening light through pewter clouds:
everywhere you're going is stone-crammed
with every place you've been: her faint-pink
blouse. . . black velvety jeans. Early Mass.
Exuberant black rubs. Roll-over comforts.

9.

Against a textured-gray resin drifter's hell. . .
a pipe corral out back, boxy plastic TV sets,
crushed green bottle glass in the carpet:
a coulees motel room. Ain't much overhead
with whiskey. . . low caliber snake-shot.

14.

Steel traps... pistols flat on dashboards.
The evening sky is pewter-mauve.
The best road in the county is slushy
where it's not snow-packed ice.
In narrow dens, coyotes curl tight.

17.

No road plowing this Monday... fresh snow
over slush. More snow. Freezing sleet.
You're driving 50, sometimes in your lane,
windows down, Jason Isbell up loud,
whiskey-hearted, rolling slick, waiting....

18.

Impassible... deep road-slush freezes overnight.
Tarot card characters... old girlfriends, drag you
off thirty-foot basalt precipices, one after another.
Alignment-hell ice ruts to and from the mailbox,
the dog chews hearing aid and genealogy ads.

20.

You sit a borrowed dream-horse, ice ride
a luminescent gray sage steppe... written off
and alone. You find a bacon-'n-grits saloon,
everyone gone with the last mangy buffalo hides.
Winter, obituary sweetheart, offers a slobbery kiss.

23.

Day is foreclosed... icy debt to signal hours.
Face south. Turn cold-north. Squint:
might be at the end of the known world,
green ocean water, last glimpse of Celtic Galicia.
No. It's coyote desert: whiskey and basalt song.

28.

Another year summoned back to Hell,
back into hiding... ancient rock-fire
in a frigid cosmos. Wild Turkey hoist,
Gaelic jig on zero-Fahrenheit blacktop:
hug the living, toast the moon-bone dead.

31.

A dog biscuit under a blue pine
marks the longer loss of a friend.
Lonesome snowy blacktop to town.
Hallucination-bark... icy spin-out.
Your spine tension-locks... you grin.

32.

Rain on six inches of old snow...
predicted to freeze on roads by dawn.
You walk the farmyard, dog-grave pine
to dog grave, your brain on heart-loss.
Motion is truth. You want to believe.

34.

The Wolfhound leads you into icy mist,
over snowy coyote tracks... westward to a lake.
Some of yesterday's slush-tracks are yours.
Freeze-crack of phone pole, *eh-caw* of crow,
mourning-green sagebrush: your heart jigs.

40.

Chuck your chewing-gum personal truths.
In the wintry north pasture, black-'n-oily
ten-foot flames, a busted old La-Z-Boy.
Heavy sleet. Fire drips onto crusted snow.
Chaucer's drunkard-ghost pukes beside you.

41.

Chunks of gristle-mutton in the restaurant
of fate... squeal of decades-gone tires:
Pacific rain on near-gone snow.
It's January... out of good cards to play,
one blood-line short of a five-line poem.

42.

No moon. Bucket-bottom darkness.
A quarter mile east, young coyotes
snap-'n-yip over a fast food snack.
Watery eyes, a farmyard-blind fool,
you pose a wish on a distant Venus.

44.

You're the meat in the meat wagon,
eighty-miles, Moses Lake to Wenatchee.
New bout: Sepsis. Gurney-strapped
you shake... icy, winter-lost silverware.
A scan presents a blocking kidney stone.

45.

A moment is how long? Kidney stone,
aging prostate, hardening of the aorta....
Slow drip of IV... Caesar Vespasian
and Doc Holliday badger Catullus
over a seedy crust of death-cold verse.

46.

You only need one kidney to live.
Chocolate shake, raspberry layer cake?
Return of rigors. An okay place to die
is downhill, a warm corner in a dead-fall
Wenatchee saloon... double whiskey ditch.

47.

First shower, half-size white hospital towels,
a nurse waits with your next Heparin shot.
Your fever is loose... wandered off for now.
It's late January. Dark cliffs, snow, ice-haze,
urethral blood in piss... needle to the belly.

48.

Beloveds not seen in rough decades
are over the crest of the next hill.
Blacktop lanes narrow. Weedy ditches.
It's simple: no more goddamn corners.
Gradually... February skies turn blue.

Straight Ahead

Straight Ahead

1.

Evening... first alfalfa cutting.
Postcard-green fields... basalt cliffs.
Back bent, you stumble a dirt road
a hundred yards, ease into a heart-safe pace,
There's a splotch-cloud summer to go.

2.

Mint jelly on tough lamb steak,
lack of cheap whiskey 'n a tent gun.
You stare-dumb at a yellow-top colony
of sweet fennel... umbrellas against grass.
It's noon... spring before carbon night.

4.

Morning corral shadows softly flutter...
cattle shipped. Thin coyote desert clouds
drift eastward. What is an accomplishment?
Bottle of beer... hot plate of canned tomales.
Early summer unpacks her dusty luggage.

5.

Nostalgia radio as bottled-tomatoes listeria...
road trip songs, brain-blood in yesterday time,
de rigueur Stetson on your thick-bone noggin'.
You roll past a sideways-growing pasture elm...
stubborn at the quickened pace of mortality.

9.

Ebony snakes in a strawberry garden....
You daydream a five-grand Platte Valley saddle.
Spring passes like some friendships... sweep
of north wind... silence on cold fort-stone.
Ahead... the broke-wing crow of six days ago.

10.

A high desert land line phone no one can repair,
cathedral perfume of sagebrush, dream departures
by amber lantern: you leash your dazzle-hound,
promise cubes of broiler pan Angus rib steak.
Obituary Tuesday... echo of graveyard wagons.

11.

One morning the outbound train tracks
are off-level, against habit, abandoned.
Buffalo stew meat on greasy old bone.
Coyote grumbles. The sky is wispy-white
against blue... a few ashy smudges.

13.

Box canyons, meteor shower blacktop roads....
You keep count with kidney-blood country music,
dented beer cans, punching bag thud-echoes.
Soon enough a headlong pitch into a grave...
perhaps to one not quite meant for you.

17.

It's just over the next sagebrush hill, a steamy bowl
of rice pilaf, yesterday's refried beans, quartered
tomatoes, crumbled burger, melted cheese slices....
Doc Holliday cough-rasps in your ear. You wake:
arthritic hands, hunger gone, no grip for pistol.

18.

Stars as small as the eye sockets of rats,
shafts of black light from black holes:
all of it wispy-hypnagogic in a blue sky.
You comb memory on spectral-quiet days,
take you bones against blood red gravity.

19.

Three years without Copenhagen Snuff.
It's a small town. A Memorial Day carnival,
a Ferris wheel, the homeless with backpacks....
Red, amber, and plum balloons curse the sky.
In the West, we waltz across shallow graves.

25.

The sun holds its tongue on the other side
of dust-tinged morning clouds. The knowing
has never been your canyon of gold nuggets.
Southbound highways, twice-steeped tea leaves,
bounce of pick-up: some luck is plowed-under.

26.

You groan at each curtain call,
the manic geared-up for self-applause.
Stopwatch in-fist, you round each corner
as if in a race, stumbling into strangers,
sometimes loved ones not seen before.

33.

Morning sunshine… a mariposa lily in bloom.
Country road apologies to the recent-dead,
you fall to splintered memory: long-haired,
short-skirted girls in raspberry rodeo shirts.
Elsewhere might only be the Ephrata Safeway.

36.

Soup-gray sundown… not a twinkle
of silver coins or a kid's starry wild rag.
Blacktop is a song for the lonesome:
midnight, no headlights, whiskey-flight.
Above the north pasture, a scream of crow.

38.

New-coat-of-paint double-wide trailers,
sweep of rain on a sage steppe road,
AM radio like lightning kill steer ribs….
You're listening: songs of the border-stranded.
Blackbird dive… fear of moonless nights.

39. *Envoi*

One lesson of our West: Bat Masterson's heart
died in New York… atop his newspaperman's desk.
A swirly pillar of rising yellow hay fire smoke…
a neighbor two miles off might see insurance bucks.
The raggedy-bereft sing cowboy songs all night long.

Deep-Lilac Heaven

To Begin With

Gilded youth... rust-colored tintypes. So went the
nineteenth century: snow on moon roses, high fives
among skeletons, dark aquamarine bone of empty
eye socket. Oh, Saint Patrick of the Wayfaring,
of the *Go-West* imperative of blood and starved
bone... such tattered monastery drapery.

The hungry drift from campfires.... Not so much
to gnaw on as a leather door hinge. Torn feather
pillows and comforters.

Gobs of ox meat... suggestion of spoiled fruit.
Slatternly large-winged, shoulder-hunched birds,
blood beaks. Long shadows of those on a trudge.

Worm-riddled Gaelic vestments... once dropped
aside on a westward trail.

Quarter-section farm dreams forsaken on dried
High Plains mud. Deer at dusk seeking water.
Handwritten letters on crumbly paper... from west
of 1844 North Platte: *Bull's Eye. We move on...
mournful.* Trees dwarf... grow bare. Disease
like belly snakes.

Omaha, Nebraska

The old stockyard corrals: splinters,
mint-flavored toothpicks, saloon sawdust.
Johnny Ringo passed through pensive-crazy.

I passed as well, once boisterous in a black
hillbilly rhinestone tuxedo jacket...
daft-'n-drunk on a delusion of poetry money.

Omaha opportunity: you could go to Bishop's
Business Equipment, buy a reconditioned Hermes
3000 Typewriter, poems embedded, fifty bucks.

You could drive west on Dodge, find a route
to Wahoo, further west and south to Fairbury.
You could cuss-vow to stay pistol-steel young.

Roadkill on the Tongue

Toss an air loop at a cedar post...
rebuild the loop. The horse
steps back, almost asleep.
The cassette on the player...
Keen's *Gringo Honeymoon.*

Bison Spoken Here is the sentiment
on a Ponca Rodeo bumper sticker.

Well-meaning don't work
the way it's supposed to.

Christ a mighty,
if you don't like this,
I explain to the horse,
think on some Parisian family
eatin' you with brussel sprouts.
He steadies-up and we rope
that post okay... sixteen-for-twenty.
Good that it ain't moving much.

Train Station Closed… Burned to the Ground

The town's lousy with fluorescent lights,
warped knotty pine coffins sloppy-stacked
behind the lone saloon… pudgy women
blustery over shrunk spines… barren wombs.

The great thing is to drink from that train
desperado's skull cup. The gnarled face mutters
like an old frontier sagwa juggler in a dream
of dancing hogs. See the banjo man hiding
in that stone church east of Scottsbluff.
Badgers-at-bay, no school after fifteen,
meth-girls at the clinic with broke ribs.

Ghost-hymns… tall High Plains grass.
I tap down on a motel clock radio.
How strange to own an old man's face,
coyote hair growing wild from big ears.

Nebraska Picture Album

Black 'n white snapshots:
a turned-over hay wagon
rotting since Roosevelt
replaced McKinley,
four-year-old Luke
riding a dry ewe
into cracked corral boards,
Kate stepping naked
from a new stock tank.

Copenhagen... Kessler's.

Maura and Ciara point
at the Milky Way,
God's eyes...
made with coyote teeth.

A closer look: the trail
Frank and Jesse James cut...
bloody, homeward from Northfield.

A green storm sky from below
the farmhouse, from a crawl space,
the sky emerald... tidal, swirling.
Snapshot: we sang *Red River Valley*
as wind and hail called our names.

Chain of Circumstance

Three moons from tourist season.
Cold beer and a cold house. I stumble
outside, jog half a football field.
At the barb wire, I shout
to ocher-blue cattle,
This is sharing!
Ice rain falls upon us.

The old desperado will bleed
just once more, so I flip the channel.
You can believe we're all on-loan,
grains of cosmic dust, even the honky tonk
girl with high-piled honey hair,
grubby hip-hugger lemon skirt.

But… tonight Baby's dark hair
spreads across my belly.
Plus we have a movie…
Sam Peckinpah horsemen
filmed at sunset… through gun oil.

Wells, Nevada

Car AC dying, you drag into town.
Earthquake: saloons and deadfall motels
flaked... crumbled like desert-dry coyote bones.

The dustiest, cheapest-ever Best Western motel,
The Sage, is empty, a cavity not quite drilled out...
no gold filling... abandoned for a decade or more.

You think to kick in a door for a noon nap.
Up Sixth, you buy a juicy cheeseburger
at Luther's, wash it down with an iced Coors.

You shamble Wells, historic district demo'd,
wonder if you'd be happy on a rocky hill
overlooking so much fibbed-'n-fabled loss.

Dark West

For dime novels
or verse of that persuasion,
Ned Buntline advised,
Work-in rancid venison,
garden corn, red-eye whiskey,
a clumsy gunfight.

Years pass like a marriage
counted in rattlesnakes
shot, chopped, butter-fried.

A century evaporates
to three years of Vegas *actresses.*

Or you drive to Tombstone for a keepsake.

Years subdivide
within battered shoeboxes:
a 19th century magnifying glass,
birth and marriage certificates
with misspelled names and places,
a miniature Bowie knife
from a Mojave street carnival.

Christmas Poem

Polished hard by December,
I walk past fake Lakota drums
in a pawnshop window.
Down the street,
a genuine bullet hole
in a cafe's wall.

Reheated Nalley's Beef Tomales
sloshing with can sauce,
plus crushed banana.
Chef's Special, $2.99.
The waitress sets a spoon
next to my hand, winks.

On AMTRAK you take what's offered
and the senator's niece got off in Milford,
because it's in Beaver County...
bought a rodeo queen belt buckle.

Better men than me
arrow-decorated bison.
I'm a chump for infatuation,
glitter tube tops and cafes
with stuffed coyotes in Plexiglas boxes.

Christmas Eve.... The waitress
says, *Jesus was a lover-boy... mischief.*

Intimate Portrait

To grow up knowing how
to hold your own death
like a library card...
and to softly place it
in a cupboard.
Perhaps field mice
would get it before
it got you. You imagined
you could learn on-the-run.

South of the Snake River

Early May… you slow-drive Lyons Ferry Road,
drought not so evident. Windows down,
you listen for ancient Nez Perce ponies.
Double-wide farmhouses… shower-damp road,
aged bloodshot eyes in the rearview mirror.

You park, walk a crushed-rock road
for a daydream. You scrawl… organize
with simple toolbox words: mint bubblegum,
back alley dice-throwing girls, Chinese ink paintings
tacked to the walls of a buckaroo's line shack.

Cafe with Slot Machines

August… there's snow
high in the Ruby Mountains.
A local rancher spots
my Copenhagen can on the counter,
says he forgot his back home.

The waitress drops a plate
of cheeseburger in front of me.
In better days she might've
kept a man. Maybe worse days.

A friend — feedlot cowboy —
guns his '76 GMC pick-up
into an ex-wife's living room,
sings *Ro-Deo-Deo Cowboy*
until the law shows up.

I'm below the snow line,
biodegradable as hell.

Hawk Season Notebook #147

Jesus in the desert. Doc Holliday in the desert. That place where madness crests... starts to recede. A trio (trinity) of coyotes accompanies each mad soul. Peregrination. Wobbly steps, thirst, wispy shapes in the distance. Dried carcasses... horse and man... the lost... those who wandered from broken down wagon or car. Beige distance. Mustardy hills. Pale yellow horizon. Failed barbed wire fences. Jesus speaks to the coyotes of his father's goldenrod sun. Doc Holliday gargles... swallows bourbon from a silver flask, speaks of being a prize-winning dental goldsmith. Was Creation in *seven days* or was it *eight* days? What is the meaning of forty desert days? As each day is peeled from its brethren, it bleeds and bleeds until it is desert-scorched, coyote gnawed white bone.

Hawk Season Notebook #348

Low autumnal sun. You wake from riding a blue horse in the Badlands of South Dakota. Glass butterflies, gigantic plastic dinosaurs on plateaus, streaking jet fighters across a deep-lilac heaven. Awake, you feel cheated of a surprise ending. The first hard freeze is about a week away. Time it right... cut the last fine sunflowers for the kitchen. Tattered forsythia-light of late September, absence of true endings, an obsession with keeping a full tank of gas: you prize the impulse... the notion of true flight.

Tonopah

Played-out hillside mine.
You cut uphill... *Private Museum.*

Wyatt Earp's hardwood toothbrush.
It's blue. Sky-blue toothbrush.
Bristles worn down in the middle.

Gingham-costumed,
a gristly schoolmarm-woman says,
Think what an Earp pistol is worth...
maybe thirty grand.

Mizpah Hotel. 1989. You rent a spot.
Brass bed. Wyatt and Sadie's room.
Rents for $27.95,
The Earp Parlor for an extra
$45, as in Colt .45.

You won't catch up:
it's fading low... the moon.

Pulling Inward

A crow sits a blackened telephone pole.
Somewhere a man with a room-size camera
and a model in an unzipped poster-red leather dress.

Last night you stared into the moon
until you heard Jesus say to Peter,
Come dine. Two coyotes and a goat.

You used to wonder how long your life would be.

Black Moon: Inward

The dead, vapor and atoms,
become self-taught drifters of the cosmic aggregate.

A rust-pocked Wyatt Earp back-in-Kansas pistol,
orgasm moan of a redhead with wavy early fifties hair,
black & white Wright Morris Nebraska photographs...
ravenous farm children... tornado-twisted towns.

Tonight's enormous sky-weight....
The past bolts-crazy into expectation of future.

About the Author

Red Shuttleworth is a three-time recipient of the Spur Award (from Western Writers of America) for Poetry: *Johnny Ringo* (2013), *Roadside Attractions* (2011) and *Western Settings* (2001). In 2016, he won the Western Heritage (Wrangler) Award for "Outstanding Poetry book" for *Woe to the Land Shadowing*. Shuttleworth was named "Best Living Western Poet" in 2007 by *True West* magazine. His poetry and short plays have appeared in numerous journals, including *Alaska Quarterly Review, Concho River Review, Los Angeles Review, Ontario Review, Prairie Schooner, South Dakota Review,* and *Weber: The Contemporary West.* Shuttleworth's plays on the West have been presented widely, including at The State University of New York at Fredonia, Sundance Playwrights Lab, The Sun Valley Festival of New Western Drama, and the Tony Award-winning Utah Shakespearean Festival.

Made in the USA
Lexington, KY
11 June 2017